The Marketing Machine® for Small Business Accountants

THE WORKBOOK

Systematic and measurable referral marketing programs

Joseph A. Krueger & Virginia S. Nicols

Dentrovisi, Inc.

Irvine, California

Copyright © 2019 by **Joseph A. Krueger & Virginia S. Nicols**

All rights reserved. No part of this publication may be reproduced, distributed or transmitted in any form or by any means, without prior written permission.

Dentrovisi, Inc.
4790 Irvine Blvd., Suite 105
Irvine, CA 92620

Book Layout © 2017 BookDesignTemplates.com

The Marketing Machine® for Professional Services THE WORKBOOK
Endless quality referrals for lawyers, accountants, consultants and more
Joseph A. Krueger & Virginia S. Nicols -- 1st ed.

ISBN: 978-1-6926535-0-7

Preface

Why a workbook for marketing professional accounting services, when we've already written an entire book?

Truthfully, we wrote this workbook in the hopes that it will force you to **work on the why and how** of your professional life.

And we purposely designed it to force you make it **your** work, emotional and physical, unimpeded by the digital interruption of the computer. There's real magic in marrying the kinetic energy of your physical handwriting with the potential energy of your mind.

The world of advertising, marketing and sales covers a broad spectrum, promoting everything from sex to ideas! It includes a huge volume of published work, from articles to white papers, books and electronic media . . . certainly in the millions of pages. (The Library at Alexandria probably included a special section on the subjects, but since it was burned we'll never know for sure!)

Certainly there is a difference between selling commodities and promoting ideas or intangibles. But there is an even more subtle **challenge to promoting the value of expertise and experience**.

In plain English, the better you are at what you do, the faster and better you do it. But not everyone values time (in particular, "your time") or the significance of creativity . . . much less the worth of good judgement. All this becomes very elusive and liquid stuff to justify in an hourly billing world.

It's easy for the experts to hypothesize on the techniques for promoting your services.

> *It's quite another thing for you to actually know the various contributing parts of your own value, much less how to describe these virtues in ways that make clients feel good (even enthusiastic?) about parting with premium dollars in exchange for your services.*

This workbook is a start on this road to discovery. Used properly (i.e. scribbled in with even the most nonsensical stuff, words crossed out or emphasized) it will become the receptacle of ideas -- the good, the bad and the unworkable.

In the final analysis the amount of effort you put into the workbook will determine its true value to your practice.

It is your work on your professional value that counts. Helping you to do it is our privilege and the reason we wrote the workbook and why it will no doubt get rewritten many times in the future.

If you follow us on the website http://AccountantsMarketingMachine.com you will get any updates you need.

Joseph Krueger

Introduction

We assume you are looking for ways to improve the profitability of your business or to make it grow. (Profitability is a requirement for growth, of course!)

Profitability can often be improved by making changes in many aspects of your business. For example, you could do a better job managing cash flow, refining your product offerings, hiring the right staff, reducing overhead, speeding up office processes, etc.

This workbook is meant to help you **focus on just one aspect of your business: improving the quality – and thus the income potential -- of the clients you serve.**

More specifically, we will be looking at ways to attract the kinds of clients you want to serve. And this only happens if they know you solve the kinds of problems they want solved!

Our book *The Marketing Machine® for Small Business Accountants* starts the process. We occasionally make reference to specific information in that book because we assume you have a copy.

But knowing something, having read it in a book, is one thing. If you want to design your customized "Machine" and actually put it to work, you'll want to take advantage of this workbook.

The workbook is meant for you to work with! You can use the workbook at the same time as you read the book, or read it by itself with an occasional look back at details in the book. In either case, have a pen in hand.

Write things down! Jot down notes, one-word reminders, or whole sentences. Highlight things you want to remember or come back to. Circle items. Use colored page markers. Place a checkbox where you want to take action.

As already said, we are big believers that physically writing things down helps memory and understanding. You can always transfer everything to digital format later.

We hope you will wear the workbook out and come to enjoy the process of doing so!

Joseph Krueger and Virginia Nicols
The Marketing Machine®

Contents

Preface i

Introduction iii

Chapter One – Understanding the Business You Are Really In 1

Chapter Two – Aren't My Credentials and Degrees My Real Marketing? 3

Chapter Three – Referrals *May* Be the Best Source of Clients 5

Chapter Four – How Do I Know Which Referrals Will Be Profitable? 7

Chapter Five – Selling Professional Services Is a Two-Phase Process 11

Chapter Six – Shaping Your Practice With A Good Marketing Plan 15

Chapter Seven – The Sales Process and The Role of Each Step 19

Chapter Eight -- Building Your Brand and Selling Into The Long Game 21

Chapter Nine – Using Direct Mail to Generate Leads and Stimulate Referrals 23

Chapter Ten – Feeding Your Referral Engine 27

Chapter Eleven – Your Website – The Hub of your Marketing Plan 33

Chapter Twelve – The Role of Publishing in Establishing Your Authority 35

Appendix One – Working with A Creative Team 37

About the Authors 41

Chapter One – Understanding the Business You Are Really In

Here are some simple questions to get started. You may be able to answer them in one sentence each. (Or not . . .!) Feel free to re-start and revise as often as necessary.

One-1: What do you want your business to achieve or accomplish **over the long term**? (What's your VISION for the business?)

_____

_____

_____

One-2: What role will sales play in helping you reach that vision?

_____

_____

One-3: Do you distinguish between sales and marketing at your firm?

_____

One-4: Describe your current sales process. Where do you think it could use improvement?

_____

One-5: Briefly describe **your current marketing** program by listing the various marketing activities you devote time and money to. (For example: print advertising, online advertising, advertising specialties like mugs and pens, networking, etc.) Give each activity a grade as to **how well you feel it performs** in attracting the right kind of business. (We're not ready yet to analyze return on investment.)

Example:

1. *Half-page ad in local business magazine. Grade: C*

Chapter Two – Aren't My Credentials and Degrees My Real Marketing?

You know the hard work that went into your studies, and the effort you put into continuing education. Our question is, "Do your clients know? Or care?"

Two-1: (a) How many framed diplomas or certificates do you have hung on the walls of your office? (b) How many professional designations do you use following your name on your business card and/or letterhead? (c) Do you have a tagline that describes in normal English what it is you actually do or specialize in?

(a)

___

(b)

___

(c)

___

Two-2: When was the last time someone approached you (in person or on the phone) saying that your formal industry credentials were what attracted her? Was it a potential client or a potential referral source? A relative? ☺ (Hint: While some will be impressed by the designations, others may be intimidated.)

___

___

___

Two-3: Our goal is to "pull" clients to you using well-designed **marketing communications.** Yes, your credentials count as one type of marketing communication .

.. but, in most cases, taken alone, are not enough. How many of the other tools listed below are you using in your current marketing and sales process?

- ☐ Informational offerings (articles, survey results, opinion pieces, etc.)
- ☐ Website designed for marketing (invite input, eMail, etc.)
- ☐ Online blog (adds up-to-date info)
- ☐ Newsletter (adds to your "authority)
- ☐ Membership program (ongoing commitment)
- ☐ Traditional printed brochure (type of format, message & graphics are key)
- ☐ Article reprints (more adding to your authority)
- ☐ Welcome and "onboarding" messages
- ☐ Regular status reports and invoices
- ☐ Other _____
- ☐ Other _____

CHAPTER THREE – REFERRALS *MAY* BE THE BEST SOURCE OF CLIENTS

Virtually every book we've seen on marketing for professionals has stressed the importance of referrals. Many books talk about referrals exclusively. We agree as to the value of referrals, but the reality is that many don't turn out to be profitable!

How you get referrals is one key to their quality. By now, you should have figured that out . . . perhaps at the expense of profits!

Chapter 3 in *The Marketing Machine® for Small Business Accountants* starts you on a clear path to getting quality referrals. (You may want to review there our definition of the different *Referral Sources*.)

Three-1: Describe your current referral program.

_____
_____
_____
_____
_____
_____

Three-2: Picture a pie chart.

(a) What percentage of the referrals you receive come from clients and other professionals, i.e., people you know personally? (Tier One) _____%

(b) What percentage of your referrals come from people you've met networking? (Tier Two) _____%

(c) What percentages of your referrals come from totally unknown sources? (Tiers Three & Four . . . "Magic Referrals") _____%

Be creative! Show the slices of your referral pie with appropriate labels.

My Referral Sources

Later, we're going to see if we can change the relative sizes of the slices of pie.

Three-3: Do you have a plan for sending something of value to people you meet at networking events? This can be an article you've written, or an article by someone else, a link to an appropriate website or something you know that relates to their interests, needs, hobbies, etc. What's the process? (Who does what to make sure follow-up contact happens?)

_____

_____

_____

Chapter Four – How Do I Know Which Referrals Will Be Profitable?

You've surely heard about "the ideal client." Naturally, you'd like your referrals to all be "ideal clients!" You won't know, though, until you've actually defined "ideal" for you and for your business. Chapter 4 gives you a process for arriving at those definitions. (Remember the exercise of sorting your clients into three or more categories? Here's more help in how to get through that sorting process.)

Four-1: Pull out a copy of your client list. Can you readily identify just by looking at the list which clients are "profitable" and which are "not profitable?"

Four-2: From your client list, pull out **a few clients you know are profitable.** What information or characteristics of these clients makes you able to make that "profitable" determination?

For example:
1. *They've been with us a long time.*
2. *They use our big-ticket services.*
3. *They are in the _____ industry, which always needs more of our help.*

Four-3: Now, look at your **full list of profitable clients**. What information can you get from your current list that helps you identify **which clients are not only profitable, but "ideal?"**

For example, does your current list show things like:

1. *Date they first became a client (Longer is usually better.)*
2. *Services used (Most profitable services?)*
3. *Information about the client business (Size, industry, distance from office)*
4. *Payment history (Pays on time; no returns)*
5. *Description of personal attributes of the client: I.Q., sense of humor, compatible political views, understands the value of time, values ideas, etc.*

List the info that your current client list contains that helps you *and anyone you would assign to this task* to know which clients are ideal.

_____
_____
_____
_____
_____
_____

Four-4: You're not looking for more referrals. You're not looking for more clients. You're looking for **more referrals of "ideal clients!"** Based on your analysis of your client list so far, how would you define the "ideal client" for your firm? We're giving you plenty of room here so you can be as specific as possible. (Hint: Knowing how to define them may not be an adequate way to describe them to others.)

Four-5: From the description above, what new categories should you add to your house list/database to include the important characteristics that make up your "ideal client?" (You can just circle them in the description.) Then take the time to add and fill in the data on your client list for these new categories. (We understand how time-consuming this could be. Be judicious in what you decide to add.)

Four-6: Re-sort your current client list for "ideal clients" and potential ideal clients. (There should be a third category, too – people who don't come near the "ideal" definition!) **How many** are there? This knowledge alone may give you an idea of why your practice hasn't yet achieved your vision.

Answers:

Ideal Clients _____   Clients w/ Potential _____   Unwanteds _____

Chapter Five – Selling Professional Services Is a Two-Phase Process

Of course there are more than two phases to selling, but we're keeping it simple here. First, for example, **you make available** an informational piece that combines what you do with some key questions that help clarify the reader's needs. Your piece attracts interest. When **someone requests the piece**, you now are "responding to their inquiry." With the questions already in their hands, it's easy for you to guide a conversation to see if you are the right person to help them. (Good questions invite thoughtful answers and let clients "sell themselves" for their ego.)

Chapter 5-1: Asking for something is tough. Giving something is easy! When you think about finding new business for the firm, do you imagine yourself "asking for something" or do you think of yourself as "finding someone new to help?" (Your answer may be very revealing!) Complete this sentence: *For me, "selling" feels like . . .*

_____

_____

Chapter 5-2: What "valuable informational pieces" do you have available for people to request?

_____

_____

_____

_____

Chapter 5-3: Do these pieces **include questions** that help begin the qualification conversation? (Remember that "She who asks the questions controls the conversation!" Always have a pocketful of questions to draw from. ☺)

Chapter 5-4: What are some of the **best qualification questions** you've found to help decide if there's a fit between the prospect and your firm's skills and services?

Chapter 5:5– How do prospects find out that these informational pieces are available? (Ads, blog posts, news releases, newsletters, social media, etc.)

Chapter 5-6: What are some more informational pieces that you could create? Should they be presented as articles? Checklists? Guides? Topics could be based on common questions/concerns/confusions you know clients cope with.

Chapter Six – Shaping Your Practice With A Good Marketing Plan

OK, this is the first real test. Do you actually have a marketing plan -- or do you believe in hope or luck as a strategy?

In Chapter 4 we focused on the client. It's equally important for your marketing plan to focus on YOU! At every step of the way your plan matches your target (read "ideal") client needs aligned with your firm's strengths.

Chapter 6-1: What is the current UVP (Unique Value Proposition) for your firm? (Personality & golf score are questionable differentiators. ☺)

_____

_____

_____

Chapter 6-2: If you don't have a UVP, you can start right here to develop one. Two simple questions can get you started:

(a) What SPECIFIC CLIENT NEED or needs stand out in your marketplace?

_____

_____

_____

(b) What makes your company UNIQUE in being able to answer that need? (Is it process, expertise, experience, resources, etc.? Hopefully, not price!)

_____

Chapter 6-3: Use this section to draft a couple of versions of a UVP based on client need and your ability to meet that need. The UVP needs to make it clear why your firm is the BEST IF NOT THE ONLY choice for the client!

This is such an important part of your marketing that we recommend you take a look at the full course we've written on developing a UVP.
(https://themarketingmachinegroup.com/zeroing-in-on-your-UVP)

Chapter 6-4: Do you have a current Marketing Plan? How often do you update it?

Chapter 6-5: What marketing **strategies** does your plan include?

Chapter 6-6: What strategies are you focusing on now?

Chapter 6-7: What marketing **tools and tactics** does your current plan include? (Here are some of the items listed in Chapter 6 of the book, to get you started: advertising, direct mail, newsletters, networking, joint ventures, public relations, pro bono work, email, social media, webinars, podcasting, search engine optimization and – your website!)

Chapter 6-8: Which of the tools and tactics have you actually put to use? Which is working the best for your current strategy?

Chapter 6-9: Do you have a schedule for introducing new strategies and/or tactics?

Chapter Seven – The Sales Process and The Role of Each Step

In the professional setting, sales can be complex and time consuming. Even in the simplest settings, you need to plan for multiple "touchpoints" with the prospective client before the sale is completed. The object of each step in the process is to get agreement to move to the next step – not to skip to the sale!

Chapter 7-1: How long is your typical sales process? (Sales cycle from the time you first get a prospect's name to the day a contract or retainer agreement is signed.)

Chapter 7-2: What are the typical steps in your current sales process? List the sales materials you use/need at each step. Every contact, including eMail, phone conversations, etc. is a separate step or touchpoint.

Remember, the goal of each step is to make a suggestion, ask a question or elaborate on an answer that segues to a subsequent step to keep the dialog going. Premature attempts to "close" can interrupt or end the process.

Take the time to come up with your complete list of steps and your description of the right collateral for that step. You may want to draw a diagram and include the number of hours, days or weeks between each step.

It's not unlikely that you will discover steps you hadn't really thought about before, and/or collateral pieces that would help get through that step and on to the next. Jot down bullet points for the content of the sales material for each step – facts, questions, calls to action, etc.

(Hint: This could be the most important exercise in the workbook!)

Describe the steps and the materials you use at each step:

_____

_____

_____

_____

_____

_____

_____

_____

Jot down here any sales materials that you realize are missing from your sequence. (Of course, not all of your "tools" will be needed in every case. But better to have them when you need them that to discover they are missing.)

_____

_____

_____

_____

_____

Chapter Eight -- Building Your Brand and Selling Into The Long Game

Your logo is NOT your brand. It is just a clever design unless it engenders a natural association with your brand. And your brand is – **whatever the consumer thinks it is!** (Repeat that thought, over, over and over again until you really believe it!) In many cases, the best way to understand and to strengthen your brand is to focus again on your UVP (Chapter 6).

Chapter 8-1: Do you have a logo?

Chapter 8-2: Was your logo designed to complement and/or represent your UVP or was it designed by a graphic artist independent of marketing research?

Chapter 8 – 3: Do you have a tagline? How well do the tagline and the logo work together to describe your company? (Note: Taglines range from one or two words to a complete sentence. In our opinion, shorter is usually better.)

Chapter 8-3: How would you define your brand? Better yet, how do you think your clients define it? How does it differentiate your firm from others in your marketplace? (Again, you may want to go back to the discussion on differentiation in Chapter 8.

And if you don't know what your clients think, here's the chance to engage them with a marketing survey!)

_____

_____

_____

_____

Chapter Nine – Using Direct Mail to Generate Leads and Stimulate Referrals

With all the work you've done so far – identifying your "ideal client," developing some marketing messages aimed at that specific type of person, and understanding the concept of "pulling" rather than "pushing" -- this chapter should make a lot of sense to you.

Direct mail is the best medium we know for personalizing your message and controlling who gets it. You can control how much information it contains, how it looks and when, where and how it will be delivered -- **unimpeded by the limitations of the delivery medium.** And mail, properly used, is perfect for "offering" something of value so that you know that, when people respond, they are likely potential clients.

Chapter 9-1: Is Direct Mail included in your marketing plan? (Whether "yes" or "no," keep working down this page to get a better understanding of how it could/should be included in your plan!)

Chapter 9-2: How many names do you have on your "List 1?" (Ideal clients) If it's fewer than 100, realize that a direct mail campaign may require that you purchase or rent outside lists.

Chapter 9-3: How often do you mail to your **ideal client**s with information **designed to help them and lead to more business for you?** (For example, announcing a developing business threat to your client's industry and offering your new service to protect against it.)

___

Chapter 9-4: Have you mailed to your list of **ideal referral sources** with information about a new service?

___

Chapter 9-5: Have you mailed to outside "cold" lists with a similar offer?

___

Chapter 9-6: What response rates have you received to your various mailings? (We're testing to see if your experience corresponds with that fictitious 2% number!)

    (a)   Offer to house list of "ideal clients." _____%
    (b)   Offer to house list of "best referral sources." _____%
    (c)   Offer to cold list. _____%

Chapter 9-7: Based on everything you've read and done so far, can you come up with **5 valuable informational "offers"** appropriate for direct mail that might generate engagement and potentially new business with **the right types of prospects**?

Just keep adding to this list as ideas come to mind. You can refine the list, the offer and the creative later!

CHAPTER TEN – FEEDING YOUR REFERRAL ENGINE

Part One – Writing

Everything you write helps establish you as an authority. And everything you write has the potential to become one of those "valuable informational pieces" that can be used as offers – on your website, in a direct mail campaign, etc.

Chapter 10-1: How would you evaluate yourself as a writer?

Chapter 10-2: What types of writing have you done or are you currently engaged in? (For example, articles on your website, guest blogs, newspaper column, LinkedIn group commentary, book, press releases, etc.)

Chapter 10-3: Do you use freelance or professional writers, editors, etc.?

Part Two – Speaking

Whenever you appear as a speaker or host, your reputation as an authority can be enhanced. (Of course it helps to have something important to say or do. ☺)

Chapter 10-4: What public appearances have you made over the past 12 months? Rate each on how effective you were as a speaker. (Poor, OK, Great)

Chapter 10-5: Go back to your previous list and rate each presentation on its effectiveness in attracting clients or client referrals. (None, 1-5, more than 5)

Chapter 10-6: Have you scheduled more appearances for the coming year?

Part Three: Pro bono work

Pro bono work can help with your marketing, or destroy your marketing plan.

Most pro bono activities have a "soft" or long-term payback that is difficult to measure. Typically, these activities will involve lending your expertise to a non-governmental charitable organization (NGO) or providing expertise and cash support to a local sports team, Rotary, Kiwanis, etc.

As a 30+ years as an active member of Rotary Clubs across the country, I know how addictive contributing to society can – and should – become. But these activities have to be balanced against your professional mental and financial wellbeing. If your income is ruled by the timeclock, no matter how rewarding the pro bono activities may be, they could endanger your fiscal health.

So what does an "Ideal" pro bono project look like for you? From our viewpoint, it should . . .

(a) Be an ongoing program with broad community benefits and wide recognition. An obscure or controversial cause can seriously hurt your brand and confuse or even alienate many in your target market.

(b) Offer you as a valuable "team member" making your professional skills available in such a way that more people will understand the benefits of using your services.

(c) Provide a "networking opportunity," a chance to make new contacts with business and community leaders who can refer clients.

Here's an example of a project that provides multiple benefits for professionals whose services include business planning, consulting, banking, financial services, insurance, etc.

The **Business Survival Project** offers helpful information to small business owners about emergency preparedness and business contingency planning – subjects becoming more important as weather disasters and man-made emergencies grow in frequency and intensity.

The program offers basic information that provokes inquiries for your business ("lead generation") and opportunities for working with business owners in a consulting capacity. See more details at http://ProfessionalsMarketingMachine.com/Business-Survival-Project/.

Chapter 10-7: Does your marketing plan include a role for pro bono activities?

Chapter 10-8: What pro bono activities from your plan are you currently taking part in? Are there any where the rewards do not seem to balance the investment?

Chapter 10-9: From your list of "not so ideal" projects above, what characteristics are missing that could turn them into "ideal" projects? How can you make those changes happen?

Part Four: Meetings, Conventions and conferences

These activities give you a unique opportunity to connect face-to-face with valuable referral sources. But if they aren't properly planned, they can waste a LOT of money!

Chapter 10-10: Does your marketing plan build in selected business meetings, seminars, conventions, etc.?

Chapter 10-11: (a) How would you rate your pre-meeting marketing planning? (b) How would you rate your at-meeting effectiveness? (How well do you stick to the plan?) (c) How about your meeting follow-up? **Give yourself a grade for each** – and then put down some suggestions for how to improve! (Appendix One in *The Marketing Machine® for Professional Services* has dozens of suggestions.)

(a) Pre-meeting Grade: _____

_____

_____

(b) At meeting Grade: _____

_____

_____

(c) Post-meeting Grade: _____

_____

_____

P.S. Meetings of your professional association are not likely to give you referrals. It probably would be more profitable to exercise your leadership skills within an organization where potential clients or referral sources are members.

Chapter Eleven – Your Website – The Hub of your Marketing Plan

You can figure that 80-90% of all referrals will check out your website before they make a decision to contact you. So your website carries a big load when it comes to your marketing! It needs to be designed with marketing in mind.

Chapter 11-1: Did you provide your website designer with marketing guidance **before** work began on the site?

Keep in mind that website designers speak in alpha-numeric code and graphic artists speak (and think) in pictures. As best we can determine, neither of these species speak with any fluency (a derivative of fluent, not to be confused with fluidity!) in terms of Marketing Strategy. If either of them took the lead in designing your website without clear and precise guidance from you or your Marketing Strategist and Copywriter you may want to revisit the site with a clear vision and set of objectives in mind.

Chapter 11-2: How successfully does your website:

- (a) Attract visitors, hold their attention and encourage return visits?
- (b) Qualify visitors by providing high-quality information **on the topics that your ideal clients are looking for?**
- (c) Describe the services you perform and your UVP?
- (d) Offer "informational pieces" that visitors can request?
- (e) Collect contact information of people who request information?

If you believe your website needs improvement, which of the categories above would be the best place to start?

_____

_____

_____

_____

Chapter 11-3: How often do you update the information on your website?

_____

Hint: The more often you post new information (i.e. blog posts, articles, announcements, etc.), the more likely people looking for that kind of information will find you through web searches.

Chapter Twelve – The Role of Publishing in Establishing Your Authority

We saved this for last, hoping not to scare you away. Delivering ideas and information by way of the written word is a disappearing art form. Kids coming out of college can barely write a coherent job description, much less compose a real resume.

As a professional, however, you are expected to have a certain level of writing skill. Every page of your website presents you as a writer and publisher – even if you don't think of yourself that way! Whatever your actual role, you need to be able to clearly convey your ideas, observations and conclusions.

The more you can communicate in your chosen profession (preferably in English, not jargon) the faster you will rise in your niche. If writing just isn't your thing, find somebody you can train to do your marketing writing for you. The more you publish (which never fully dies on the web), the faster you will achieve authority status.

At some point (the sooner the better) you want to be thinking about publishing your story about your professional pursuits . . . your "authority book!"

Chapter 12-1: How do you rate your own writing ability when it comes to professional topics?

Chapter 12-2: Do you regularly use proof-readers for your professional writings? What about editors?

Chapter 12-3: Have you considered the services of a speechwriter or consultant for major presentations?

Chapter 12-4: Have you considered the value of a book to boost your reputation as an authority? What is standing in your way?

(If you don't know how to get started, send us an email and ask for our *Book Writer's Start-up Kit!*)

Chapter 12-5: When would you like to have your book published? (A leading question if ever there was one!)

Appendix One – Working with a Creative Team

If you've actually done the exercises here in The Workbook, you will be inspired – even compelled! – to evaluate how well your marketing pieces are working for you. We trust you have come up with some ideas for improving them!

Each marketing piece has a different purpose, as we have described. Still, you probably want all of them to have the same, or at least a similar "look and feel" to help strengthen your brand.

"Look and feel" involves design, colors, typography (fonts), layout, copywriting (tone, word choice), format, paper choice, etc., etc. In other words, it's a whole "family" world filled with professional designers, artists and writers!

Still, you are the boss. This is your project, so **you have to lay the groundwork** so each marketing piece performs the way it's meant to. You do that via a **Creative Work Plan.**

On the next page we've included a generic Creative Work Plan that can be used for each piece of marketing collateral you decide you need. Feel free to expand; be careful before you delete any of the items.

We recommend you make a separate plan for each piece of collateral, then go over it with your creative team member/s to be sure everyone is in agreement before any work begins.

(***An aside from Virginia.*** In the years of my working as a direct response copywriter for some very large multinational corporations, it wasn't unusual for the

Creative Work Plan to be a much longer document than the finished piece! I remember one Plan that was 8 pages of closely typed information to guide the writing for a simple brochure that had maybe 350 words on it! We learned over and over again that the better the direction, the fewer the disappointments and the less time spent on do-overs.)

CREATIVE WORK PLAN

Program, item (format of finished piece)

_____

Date_____ Creative Team_____

1-Program objectives (*see notes*)

_____

2-Background

_____

3-Description of product/service being offered (*see notes*)

_____

4-Target market audience (decision maker)

_____

5-Scope of work (direct mail letter, article reprint, etc.)

_____

6-Offer (What do, what get?) (*see notes*)

_____

7-Call to Action

_____

8-Key copy points

_____

9-Key graphic points (mandatories) (*see notes*)

_____

10-Tone & manner (*see notes*)

_____

11-Budget/schedule

_____

Notes:

Program vs. product vs. offer. The program would be your current marketing campaign aimed, for example, at bringing in new business from existing clients. The product would be the upcoming seminar introducing a service you've recently added to your portfolio. The offer is what the person gets by responding to the Call to Action on this piece. ("Call now to reserve a seat at the upcoming seminar.")

Mandatories are the items that need to be included on the piece, whether printed or digital, such as the logo, a copyright line, privacy statement, date, etc.

Tone and Manner are decided in large part by the person who is the "author" of the piece. A message written by the office manager, for example, would have a different tone and manner than a message coming from the President or principal of the firm.

About the Authors

Joe Krueger and Virginia Nicols

If you haven't figured it out by now, we have been in the marketing and publishing business for quite a while. When you combine all our experience, it totals to over 50 years!

It's treated us well — and we still like it and write every day!

We are actively looking for projects where we can bring our collective body of marketing experience to bear, whether it's helping a sole practitioner break through to a new level of success, or whether it's helping a whole neighborhood organize itself to prepare for disasters. (Look for some of our published works on emergency preparedness on Amazon!)

One thing we've learned is that people want information and help not necessarily when they need it, but when they want it! To that end, we try to make some training materials available for whenever the impulse hits.

At our website https://TheMarketingMachineGroup.com you'll find a collection of downloadable articles and courses for sale. Since you've already read this book you may want to take a look at these courses, in particular:

- Be a Power Presenter!
- Website – The Hub of Your Marketing Plan
- Better eMail Copy
- Strategic Marketing Plan for Professionals
- Professional Networking Guide

You can download these marketing materials anytime, day or night. Each course is easy to read, in step-by-step format, and comes with a workbook.

Finally, we are particularly eager to help people who are ready to take the next step toward publishing their authority book. Part of our service is personal consulting to get you off to a solid start. Naturally, we only offer consulting to a limited number of people, so if you think you'll be interested, **request the Book-Writing Start-Up Kit now** to get to the top of the list. We look forward to hearing from you!

Joe

http://JosephKrueger.com/contact

Virginia

http://VirginiaNicols.com/contact

P.S. Thanks in advance for comments at our site and reviews of our books on Amazon. Your personal involvement can help us improve our materials and reach more people.

www.ingramcontent.com/pod-product-compliance
Lightning Source LLC
Chambersburg PA
CBHW080910220526
45466CB00011BA/3534